ACTIVE PARENTING PRE AND POST RELEASE

REENTRY
ESSENTIALS, INC.

Life Skills Series
Basic Skills for Lifelong Success

Reentry Essentials, Inc.
98 4th Street, Suite 414
Brooklyn, NY 11231
P: 347.973.0004
E: info@ReentryEssentials.org
I: www.ReentryEssentials.org

This workbook belongs to:

_____

You may find it helpful to keep important names and phone numbers handy.

Write them below.

Child's caregiver

Name_____

Phone_____

Probation officer

Name_____

Phone_____

Parole officer

Name_____

Phone_____

Social services

Name_____

Phone_____

Child support office

Name_____

Phone_____

Other important numbers

_____
_____
_____
_____
_____
_____

IF YOU ARE A PARENT CURRENTLY IN PRISON OR WERE RECENTLY RELEASED. THIS WORKBOOK IS FOR YOU.

It can help you:

Stay connected with your child

You can do this by:

- staying in regular contact
- keeping track of your child's education

Become more involved in raising your child after release

- It will be a new chance for you to be there
- for your child as he or she grows up.

Work on being the best parent you can be

There are many skills involved in parenting. You can work on the skills you have, and learn new ones. All it takes is effort and commitment.

You can still play an important role in your child's life.

CONTENT

CAN YOU BE AN EFFECTIVE PARENT WHEN YOU ARE IN PRISON?
The answer is yes. But you will face some challenges.

Being away from your child is a challenge.

You won't be able to provide for your child. You also won't be able to see him or her every day. You won't be able to be there to celebrate accomplishments and help your child learn and grow. But you can still be a part of your child's life. This involves:

- making the most of the contact you do have with your child
- being honest with him or her
- sharing thoughts and feelings
- learning all you can about
- what's going on in your child's life
- staying involved in your child's education as much as you can

Your child is being raised by someone else.

The caregiver may be your current partner, a former partner, the child's grandparent or a foster parent. You may or may not currently have a good relationship with the child's caregiver.

To be an effective parent in prison, you will need to:

- set aside negative feelings you have for the caregiver, if any
- treat him or her with respect
- ask for the caregivers help to stay in touch with your child
- work with the caregiver on what's best for your child

Your sentence affects your child, too.

He or she will miss you. But your child may also face teasing from other children about your prison term. This could lead to many feelings, such as anger, in your child.

Your child may not want to have much to do with you at first. But if you respect your child's feelings and work on his or her terms, you can take steps to improve your relationship.

Pledge to make any changes needed to be a better parent. Your child needs you!

YOUR CHILD WILL HAVE QUESTIONS.

Be as honest as you can in your replies. Here are some common questions children ask, with tips on answering them.

"What is prison?"

If your child is young, he or she may not even know what prison is. Explain that prison is a place some adults have to go to when they break the rules (law).

"Why are you there?"

Explain that you made a mistake, and that you are taking responsibility for your actions. Don't get into details about your crime for younger children, but give a brief explanation. For example, "I hurt someone," or "I sold something that is not allowed." If your child is older, he or she may have more questions. Answer them as honestly as you can.

"How long will you be there?"

Tell your child when your sentence is scheduled to end. If you will be eligible for parole, explain that you may be able to come home earlier. But don't make any promises. Don't say you'll be home "soon," if you still have a lot of time left in your sentence.

"Are you OK?"

It's important for your child to know that you are safe. If your child visits you, he or she will be able to tell it's not a nice place to be. Don't give your child the idea that you are in a good place. But reassure him or her that you are safe there.

"What is prison like?"

You can tell your child:

- what you eat
- what you wear
- where you sleep
- about the facilities in the prison (for example, TV room, library, showers and the yard)
- when you wake up and go to bed
- when you exercise
- how you spend your day, including any jobs you do or classes you take

"Is it my fault?"

Children may feel guilty that you are in a corrections facility, and think that they made it happen somehow. Help your child understand that you are not in prison because of anything he or she did. Make it clear that you are the one who did something wrong, and nobody else.

"Will I go to prison when I grow up?"

Children may be afraid that they will end up in prison just like you. Explain to your child that only people who break the law have to go to prison.

"What will happen to me?"

Your child may wonder what things will be like when you are not around. Explain:

- what your child's living arrangements will be
- who his or her caregiver will be
- any changes this involves (such as moving to a new place)

Reassure your child that he or she will be OK.

STAY IN TOUCH WITH YOUR CHILD REGULARLY.

Take responsibility for staying in contact with your child.
Don't wait for your child to contact you.

Write to your child often.

- Always mention how much you love and miss him or her.
- Encourage your child to write back to you. Ask him or her to send along photos, drawings and copies of schoolwork.
- Ask questions when you write— for example, about your child's school, friends or pets.
- Send younger children many short letters or notes. Print with large, clear letters. Ask the caregiver to read the letters aloud, if needed.
- If your child can't write, ask the caregiver to write out your child's messages to you.
- For an older child or teen, share memories—about your child, or about when you were his or her age.
- Be sure to write before any special occasions, such as your child's birthday.
- Consider a drawing activity if your child is young. Start a drawing and mail it your child. Ask the child to add to the drawing, and then send it back.
- Be sure to follow all the rules at your facility for sending and receiving mail (including e-mail, if your facility allows it).

Make phone calls when you can.

- Arrange a time when you can use a phone and your child will be home.
- Ask your child questions, but don't push any topics that he or she doesn't seem comfortable talking about.
- Ask about getting a prepaid inmate calling card, to avoid calling your loved ones collect.
- Be sure to follow all the rules at your facility for making phone calls. These may include limits on when you can use the phone and for how long. There may also be rules about what you can discuss.

If possible, arrange for your child to visit you.

Work out the details with your child's caregiver. Remember, your child may find your facility a scary place. He or she may not feel like talking much. But that's OK—the important thing is that you get to spend time together.

Don't give up!

Even if you don't hear back from your child, keep trying to get in touch. It helps show you care.

WRITE DOWN CONTACT INFORMATION FOR YOUR CHILDREN HERE.

	Child #1	Child #2	Child #3	Child #4
Name				
Caregiver				
Address and e-mail				
Phone number				
Best time to call				
Birthday				
Notes				

KEEP THE CONVERSATION GOING WITH YOUR CHILD
Here are some tips on interacting with your child in letters, phone calls and visits.

Talk about your child's interests.

For example, you can talk about his or her:

- favorite TV show
- favorite book
- friends
- family members

Ask about your child's day.

For example, you can ask about:

- what your child did
- what your child ate
- places your child went
- events your child attended

Talk about your day.

Let your child know how you spent your time. You can tell him or her about:

- any classes you take
- what you had for lunch
- what you did for work

Share experiences.

- Watch the same TV show or sporting event.
- Read a book your child is reading.
- Read short passages from a favorite book to him or her over the phone.

Play games.

- Start telling a story, and ask your child to continue it.
- Use letters to play a game by mail—such as tic-tac-toe.

Take part in parenting programs.

Some facilities have programs that allow parents to record audio or video messages for their children. Ask if your facility has any programs like this.

Make the most of visits.

- If your child is an infant, play games such as peek a- boo or patty-cake.
- If your child wants to talk, be a good listener.
- Draw pictures together.
- Read your child a story.
- Play a game together, such as "I spy." Or play a game your facility lets families use during visits.
- Ask about things that are going on in your child's life.
- Tell your child you love him or her.

Write some other ideas below:

_____

_____

_____

_____

_____

_____

_____

_____

Be sure to follow your facility's rules for interacting with visitors.

KEEP A JOURNAL.
This can help you cope with the separation from your child.
You can write about whatever you want, including:

Thoughts and feelings

These may include:

- thoughts on your situation
- feelings toward your child
- feelings about being separated from your child
- your daily life in the facility
- lessons you've learned
- regrets for how your child has been affected by your actions

Ways you can stay connected

These could involve:

- ideas on what to talk about with your child
- questions you want to ask your child
- conversations you want to have with your child's caregiver

Future plans

These may include:

- things you want to do with your child after your release dreams you have for your child (such as watching him or her graduate from college)
- completing your education
- ways you can be a better parent

Practice right now.

Write down what's on your mind below. (Later, you might want to start keeping your journal in a bound notebook. Follow facility guidelines for the type of notebook allowed.)

_____

_____

_____

_____

_____

_____

_____

_____

_____

_____

_____

_____

_____

_____

_____

_____

GET STARTED TODAY.

Use this form to write a letter to your child. Start by writing about something you thought of today (for example, something you and your child did together in the past).

Date: _____

Dear _____

Today, I

_____

_____

_____

_____

_____

_____

_____

_____

_____

_____

_____

_____

_____

_____

_____

_____

_____

_____

_____

Here is something I want to share with you.

I though it was

_____

_____

_____

_____

(Attach a cartoon or photograph from a newspaper or magazine, for example.)

RESPECT YOU CHILD'S FEELINGS.

Your child loves you, but he or she may be having trouble coping with your sentence.

Your child may have many different feelings.

He or she may feel:

- angry
- abandoned
- sad
- worried
- confused
- frustrated
- guilty
- tense
- afraid
- ashamed

All of these feelings are normal.

Talk with your child about these feelings.

Encourage him or her to share these feelings with you. Explain that it's OK to have those feelings. Reassure your child that you love him or her no matter what. And remind your child that he or she is not responsible in any way for your being in the correctional facility.

Encourage your child to find an outlet for these feelings.

For example, to manage feelings, he or she can:

- draw
- keep a diary or journal
- listen to music
- talk to a trusted adult

For feelings of anger or frustration especially, suggest counting to ten, or taking several slow, deep breaths.

Share your feelings, too.

For example, you can talk about how you feel about what you did. Or you can tell your child that it makes you sad when you can't see him or her. And you can remind your child that you love him or her very much.

Talk with your child's caregiver.

Ask him or her to watch for signs that your child is having trouble managing feelings.

These signs may include:

- withdrawal from people or activities
- bed wetting (after child has learned to stay dry)
- lack of interest in other people
- low self-esteem
- falling grades
- frequent or severe temper tantrums
- fighting
- physical problems (such as trouble sleeping, headaches or stomachaches)

Encourage your child's caregiver to talk to your child about feelings often. Ask him or her to consider talking to your child's health-care provider or school counselor if these signs seem severe or last a long time.

STAY INVOLVED IN YOUR CHILD'S EDUCATION AS MUCH AS YOU CAN.

You can't be with your child every day. But you can still help him or her be successful in school.

Always ask your child about school.

You can start the conversation by asking, "How's school?" But don't stop there. Ask about your child's assignments, report cards and how he or she did on tests. Other questions you could ask:

- "What were the best and worst parts of your day?"
- "Which subject do you like the most (and least)?"
- "What did you do in class today?"

Encourage good study habits.

Talk with your child's caregiver about setting rules for your child's homework. Encourage him or her to set up a study space and a time for doing homework each night.

Talk with your child about the importance of homework and always doing his or her best. Encourage him or her to ask the caregiver or a teacher for help, if needed.

Help build your child's self-esteem and confidence.

For example, you can:

- encourage him or her to get involved in school activities
- give praise when your child does well on a test

If your child doesn't do well on a test, don't criticize. Talk about ways he or she can do better next time.

Try to get copies of your child's work.

Ask your child's caregiver if he or she will make copies of:

- graded tests
- assignments
- other projects

If you want to learn more about a subject your child is taking, check your facility's library.

Help your child set goals.

Ask your child what he or she would like to do in the next few months. For example, he or she might want to:

- get a better grade
- join a club
- try out for a play

Talk about steps your child can take to reach these goals.

Stay on top of your child's school schedule.

Use the space on the next page to keep track of this information. (Ask the child's caregiver for help.) Learn about your child's:

- teachers
- friends
- schedule
- homework assignments
- tests, including standardized tests

USE THIS CHART TO KEEP TRACK OF YOUR CHILD'S TIME IN SCHOOL.

School information:

- Name of school:

  _____

- Address:

  _____

  _____

- Child's teacher(s):

  _____

  _____

  _____

- School principal:

  _____

Notes (friends, activities, etc.)

_____

_____

_____

_____

_____

_____

_____

_____

_____

_____

_____

_____

_____

Grades:

Subject	Date	Description	Grade

Standardized Tests/State Tests:

Name	Date/Time	Score

WORK ON A GOOD RELATIONSHIP WITH YOUR CHILD'S CAREGIVER.

It's important if you want to stay connected with your child and be an involved parent.

Remember, the caregiver is your connection to your child.

He or she is responsible for raising your child and providing for your child's needs. Always keep that in mind, whether the caregiver is your:

- current spouse or partner
- former spouse or partner
- parent
- other relative
- foster parent

Whatever has happened between you and the caregiver, leave the past in the past. Focus on what's best for your child.

Always treat your child's caregiver with respect.

In general:

- Treat the caregiver the way you would like to be treated.
- Don't yell or raise your voice.
- Don't bring up things that happened in the past.
- Don't blame or criticize the caregiver.

Ask the caregiver to treat you with respect.

The caregiver may have negative feelings toward you. Encourage him or her to discuss those feelings, and listen. Explain that you understand those feelings, but that you just want to do what's best for your child.

Be polite to each other in front of your child.

If you are having a conflict with the caregiver, talk about it in private. Discussing it in front of your child will only make things more stressful for him or her. Don't display any negative feelings toward the caregiver, even if you are angry.

Don't use your child as a messenger.

If you have anything to say to the caregiver, say it directly to that person. Don't ask your child to pass along a message.

Don't say bad things about the caregiver to your child.

If you have negative feelings toward the caregiver, there's no need to tell your child. Doing so will only make him or her upset. Remember, your child lives with the caregiver. It's important for your child to feel that everything is OK between you.

Make your intentions clear.

- Tell the caregiver that you want to stay involved in your child's life as much as possible.
- Make it clear that you are willing to work with the caregiver to do what's best for your child.
- Consider taking a parenting class, if your facility offers one.

Ask for the caregivers help.

- Ask him or her to encourage your child to respond to letters you send, and to take your phone calls.
- If your child is very young, ask the caregiver to help him or her write letters to you.
- Ask the caregiver for photos of special events your child is involved in.
- Ask to be told about any developments or problems involving your child—at school or at home.

Agree that your child's needs come first.

Be willing to set aside any differences you have with the caregiver to focus on what's best for your child. Also be willing to make any changes needed.

How can you improve your relationship with your child's caregiver?

Write your ideas below.

_____
_____
_____
_____
_____
_____
_____
_____
_____
_____
_____
_____
_____
_____
_____
_____
_____
_____

Even if you are in a positive, loving relationship with your child's caregiver, you still need to make the effort to be involved in your child's day-to-day life.

WHEN YOU ARE RELEASED
Take steps so you can be there for your child.

Think of your release as a new beginning.

This is a chance to rebuild your life and to be a better parent for your child. Building a new life means making changes. This could involve giving up old habits and even old friends.

Take it slow.

It will take time to put your new life together. You won't be able to do everything at once. Focus on one thing at a time, one day at a time.

Stay positive.

Starting over may seem challenging. But lots of people have done it, and you can, too. Remember, everybody has setbacks and bad days. But if you keep working on making positive changes in your life, it will pay off. Keep yourself busy for example, with school, work and volunteering.

Remember that your actions are important.

They could determine your visitation rights and whether or not you get custody of your child. If you are paroled, taking the right steps is very important.

Follow your pre-release plan.

- If you are paroled, make sure you understand the conditions, and follow them. Stay in contact with your parole officer.
- If you've had problems with alcohol or other drug use, consider a treatment program or support group.

Build a support system.

- Reach out to friends and family members who are positive influences.
- Stay away from old friends who are negative influences, or who take part in criminal behavior.
- Get involved in a community or church group.

Write down things you'll need to do first after your release:

_____

_____

_____

_____

_____

_____

_____

_____

_____

_____

_____

_____

_____

_____

_____

_____

_____

_____

_____

_____

_____

_____

_____

KEEP YOUR EXPECTATIONS REASONABLE.

Being released is something to feel good about! But don't expect things to go back to the way they were before you went to a correctional facility.

Your child may have mixed feelings.

Remember, your child has been used to limited contact with you. He or she may be happy you are out, but may also wonder what's going to happen. (See page 19 for some common reactions children have after being separated from a parent.)

You may have mixed feelings, too.

Things may not seem the same as before you went into prison. That's because things aren't the same. Your loved ones have changed during that time—and so have you.

Resist thinking about the time you've lost or the things you don't have. Instead, focus on the opportunity to start over. This includes the opportunity to become more involved in your child's life.

Take things slowly with your child.

Arrange for regular visits, but don't try to change your child's routine too much. If you are seeking custody, keep in mind that it may take some time.

Be honest with others and yourself.

- Accept that spending time in prison may limit the opportunities you have for jobs and places to live. Make the most of the opportunities you do have.
- Don't make promises you can't keep.
- Ask for help if you need it.

Give things time.

It will take a while for your family, including your child, to adjust to your being out of prison. It will take time for you to adjust, too.

What are your expectations after release?

Write them below.

_____

_____

_____

_____

_____

_____

_____

_____

_____

_____

_____

_____

_____

_____

_____

_____

_____

_____

_____

_____

SET SOME GOALS.

Keep them practical and realistic. Make a plan for reaching the goals you set.

Personal goals

These may include:

- building a better relationship with your child
- spending time regularly with your child
- becoming a better parent
- joining a church or support group

Practical goals

Some examples include:

- finding a place to live
- getting a car

Professional goals

For example, you may want to:

- get a steady job as soon as you can
- enroll in a training program

Educational goals

You may want to:

- take classes
- work toward getting a degree

Short-term goals

(things I want to do in the next few days or weeks)

_____

_____

_____

_____

_____

Medium-term goals

(things I want to do in the next few months)

_____

_____

_____

_____

Long-term goals

(things I want to do in the next few years)

_____

_____

_____

_____

_____

_____

ADJUSTING TO CHANGE CAN BE CHALLENGING.
But it's also an opportunity to improve yourself.

Your child has been living with someone else.

Depending on your situation, this may continue to be the case. Avoid criticizing your child and his or her caregiver. They did the best they could while you were serving your time.

While you were away, your child looked to the caregiver for guidance and support. You can play a greater role in your child's life, but you will have to earn back everyone's trust.

Your family has learned to live without you.

If you were the head of the household before, don't expect to step right back into that role. You have to prove that you have changed and are dependable.

If you won't be living with your family, it will take time for you to become part of their lives again.

Remember that things won't go back to the way they were.

You may want things to get back to normal after your release. That's not likely to happen, but that's OK You'll find a "new normal." You may get a new:

- job
- place to live
- partner

But your child can be a big part of your new life.

Take steps to help you stay out of prison.

Avoid old habits and old friends that had anything to do with the crime that landed you in prison. There's a very good chance they would help send you back. See page 29 for sources of help, if you need them.

What are some changes you've noticed?

Write down anything that seems different to you since you've been out:

_____

_____

_____

_____

_____

_____

_____

_____

_____

_____

_____

_____

_____

_____

_____

_____

_____

HOW YOUR CHILD REACTS TO YOUR RELEASE

Depends on your relationship with him or her, and how long you were away. But here are some common reactions you can expect.

Infants

Even if your sentence was short, and your child is still an infant, he or she will not recognize you. In fact, your child may react as if you are a stranger. He or she may:

- cry
- not want you to hold him or her
- cling to the caregiver

Toddlers

If your child is a toddler, he or she may:

- act shy around you (especially if he or she was unable to visit you)
- seem to not recognize you
- cry
- throw tantrums
- cling to the caregiver

Preschoolers

A child this age may:

- seek all your attention
- be angry with you for going away
- blame him or herself for your prison term
- test limits
- be eager to tell you about things that happened while you were away

Older children

If you had a good relationship with your child before, he or she will likely be happy to see you. Your child may seek all your attention. He or she may want to talk to you about school or other topics.

If you didn't have a good relationship with your child before, he or she may seem withdrawn.

Teens

A child this age is already going through a lot of changes. He or she may:

- have mixed feelings about your being back
- seem excited to see you, or act withdrawn
- wonder what's going to happen now that you are out
- feel uncomfortable expressing feelings

How did your child react?

Write down what happened:

_____

_____

_____

_____

_____

_____

_____

_____

_____

_____

_____

_____

_____

_____

SPEND TIME WITH YOUR CHILD.

The more time you spend with your child, the closer you will become.
Here are some tips for developing a closer relationship.

Infants

Hold and touch your baby. Play simple games, such as peek-a-boo. If you live with your child, get involved with his or her daily care—such as feedings or changing diapers.

Toddlers

It's important to be gentle and loving. When talking with your child, sit or kneel down so that you are at eye level. This will seem less threatening.

Preschoolers

Reassure your child it wasn't his or her fault that you had to go away. Play fun games together. Avoid discipline at first.

(See pages 21 and 25 for more on disciplining your child.)

Older children

Give your child lots of love and attention. Continue to keep track of how your child is doing in school. Praise your child's accomplishments, and let him or her know how proud you are. Don't criticize your child, and avoid disciplining at first.

Teens

Teens are very sensitive to criticism and teasing, so it's best to avoid those behaviors. Your child may be withdrawn. Ask him or her questions about what's going on in his or her life. You can also ask about how he or she feels about your release. Accept your teen's feelings, whatever they are.

Do fun things together.

For example, you could take your child to:

- the park
- the library
- a museum
- a movie

Write down some things you can do with your child:

_____
_____
_____
_____
_____
_____
_____
_____
_____
_____
_____
_____
_____
_____
_____
_____
_____
_____
_____

CONTINUE TO WORK WITH YOUR CHILD'S CAREGIVER.

Whatever your situation, talk about ways you can take on more parenting responsibilities.

Arrange times to see your child.

If you're not living with your child, don't drop by unannounced. Talk with your child's caregiver ahead of time about when you can visit or spend time with your child.

Work out financial responsibilities.

There are many costs involved in raising a child. As soon as you get a job, work out a family budget or a payment plan to help cover the costs of:

- clothing and food
- school supplies
- health care
- child care (day-care centers or baby sitters, for example)
- long-term savings (a college fund, for example)
- any child support you owe

Talk about making decisions.

It's important to be effective "co-parents" for your child's sake. Discuss how you will make decisions about your child. Some may be done together—for example, decisions about discipline. If you live apart from your child, other decisions may be made by the caregiver alone—mealtimes and study time, for example.

Discuss morals and values.

For example, you might want to talk about:

- how you will each teach your child important values (such as respect, responsibility and honesty)
- where and how your child will worship
- what forms of entertainment are acceptable for your child

Work out a plan for special occasions.

Make a schedule ahead of time. Talk about plans for:

- birthdays
- holidays
- vacations

Respect the caregivers' rules.

For example, he or she may have rules about your child's bedtime or diet. Support these decisions to help keep things consistent for your child.

Be ready for unexpected changes.

For example, your child may get sick or may need a ride. Be ready to help out when needed.

Take it slowly as you readjust to family life.

If you are living with your child and his or her caregiver, getting to know each other again will take some time. Be patient— and get help if needed.

IF YOU GET CUSTODY OF YOUR CHILD.

Here are some tips on learning to live together again.

Keep your child's caregiver involved in your child's life.

Work out times when the caregiver can visit your child or spend time with him or her. Invite the caregiver to birthday parties and other special occasions.

Don't be jealous of your child's time with the caregiver.

Your child may miss the caregiver and have mixed feelings about living with you again. Respect these feelings, and encourage your child to talk about them.

Transition your child slowly.

Remember, your child has been used to living in a different home, with a different set of rules. Consider following the caregivers rules at first. Work in rules you have little by little.

Let your child help with decisions.

This can help him or her feel responsible and part of the household. Depending on your child's age, he or she can decide on:

- what to have for dinner
- chores he or she can do
- a fun thing you can do together, such as going for a walk or reading

Be patient.

It will take time for you and your child to get used to living together again. Things won't always go smoothly. If you are having problems, reach out to your support system. (See page 15.)

What are some ways you can be a family again?

Write your ideas below.

_____

_____

_____

_____

_____

_____

_____

_____

_____

_____

_____

_____

_____

_____

_____

_____

_____

_____

_____

_____

IMPROVE YOUR COMMUNICATION SKILLS.

This can help you work with your child's caregiver more effectively. It can also help you be a better parent.

Know what good communication is.

Good communication means.

- sharing your own feelings
- listening to the other person
- solving conflicts and working out solutions to problems

Be willing to share your thoughts and feelings.

You may find it hard to open up at first. At times, it may seem as if nobody understands what you went through.

But remember that your time in the correctional facility affected the whole family, including your child. Your family had to learn to get by without you. And your child may have been teased at school. Your time in prison is something you all had to deal with.

Be a good listener.

Here are some ways to let a person know you are interested in what he or she has to say:

- Maintain eye contact.
- Ignore distractions while the other person is speaking.
- Don't interrupt.
- Don't overreact to anything the person says.
- Pay attention to the person's body language and tone of voice. They can give you clues on how he or she really feels.
- Restate what the person told you in your own words, to show that you understand.
- Ask open-ended questions, rather than questions that can be answered with "yes" or "no." For example, you could ask, "How do you feel about that?" instead of "Are you angry?"

Create win-win situations.

If you are having a conflict with the child's caregiver, try to solve it. First, figure out what the problem is. Together, think of different ways you could solve the problem. Come up with as many different possible solutions as you can. Choose the one you think will work best for both of you, then try it out. If it doesn't work, try another solution.

Don't make it personal.

Remember, the problem is not your child's caregiver. The problem is the conflict you are having. Keep the discussion focused on the conflict. Keep your feelings about the caregiver out of it.

Don't criticize or judge.

You may not approve of the way the caregiver handled certain things while you were gone. But criticizing won't help anything. It will only make the caregiver angry, and could make it more difficult for you to spend time with your child.

Accept that the caregiver did the best he or she could. Leave the past behind. Focus on decisions you need to make right now. If there is an unresolved conflict you'd like to talk about, deal with it another time.

Use "I" statements.

This is a way of telling someone how you feel without placing any blame. Placing blame only makes a person defensive, and gets in the way of communication.

For example, saying, "You never tell me anything!" places blame on the other person. A more effective statement is "I get upset when you don't tell me things that involve my child."

Practice using "I" statements.

Think of a conflict you are having with your child's caregiver. How can you phrase it as an "I" statement?

Write it below.

_____

_____

_____

_____

_____

_____

_____

_____

_____

_____

_____

_____

_____

_____

_____

_____

_____

_____

_____

_____

_____

_____

_____

FOCUS ON BEING THE BEST PARENT YOU CAN BE.
It will take patience, planning and practice.

Express your love for your child often.

Tell your child regularly that you love him or her. You can also show your love by:

- holding him or her
- smiling
- sharing your time
- listening
- staying involved in your child's life

Help build your child's self-confidence and independence.

- Let your child try new things that are appropriate for his or her age.
- Give your child responsibilities, such as chores. For example, he or she can be in charge of feeding a pet, or clearing off the table after dinner.

Use loving discipline with your child.

Work with your child's caregiver on discipline and agree on the methods you'll use in general:

- Set some rules your child must follow. Also set consequences for breaking those rules. Make sure your child understands both.
- If your child breaks a rule, put the consequence into effect right away. Be sure to stay calm. Don't call your child names or yell.
- Be consistent and fair. Make sure the consequences fit the action. For example, if your child doesn't put a toy away, say he or she can't play with it for a short time.
- Praise your child when you see him or her being good. Be specific about the behavior you liked.
- Never spank your child or use any form of physical punishment.

Use discipline methods that are appropriate for your child's age.

- Hold your child and say "no" calmly but firmly. Don't yell. Or redirect children younger than 2 from unsafe or unwanted activity.
- If your toddler has a tantrum, stay cool and wait for it to pass. Don't reward the tantrum with your attention.
- Consider "timeouts" for children ages 3 and 4. Have your child sit quietly for a minute or two in a place where there are no distractions.
- If your child is between the ages of 5 and 10, explain the reasons for rules. For example, say "You have to go to bed at this time so you'll have enough rest for school tomorrow."
- Adjust rules as needed for preteens and teens. For example, you can set a curfew.

Be a good role model.

Your child learns a lot about how to interact with other people by watching you.

- Show respect for your child and for others.
- Treat other people fairly.
- Approach problems with a positive attitude.
- Demonstrate good values, such as honesty, responsibility and hard work.

Talk to your child each day.

Give your child at least 5 minutes of your undivided attention each day, if possible. If your child doesn't live with you, stay in touch each day through a short phone call. (Be sure to arrange this with the child's caregiver first.)

Be a positive influence in your child's life.

- Take part in your child's activities.
- Let your child know that you will always be there for him or her.
- Keep your child away from people in your past who were negative influences.
- If your child is old enough, talk about your prison term. Explain that what you did was wrong, and that you have learned from your mistake.

What are some things you will do to become a better parent?

Write them below.

_____

_____

_____

_____

_____

_____

_____

_____

_____

_____

_____

_____

_____

_____

_____

_____

_____

_____

_____

_____

_____

_____

_____

TAKE CARE OF YOURSELF.
Follow these tips on staying healthy.

Find healthy ways to deal with stress.

- Recognize when you are feeling stressed. Common signs include tight muscles, headaches and getting upset over things that usually don't bother you.
- Continue to keep a journal of your thoughts and feelings.
- Set priorities, and focus on getting the most important things done first.
- Accept what you can't control. For example, if there's a long line at the store, there's nothing you can do about that. But you can control how you react. Stay calm.
- Try to think positively. Tell yourself you can handle the situation. Keep things in perspective.
- Spend some time each day on a hobby or other fun activity.
- Consider a relaxation technique, such as deep breathing. Take several slow, deep breaths.
- Try progressive muscle relaxation. Sit or lie down. Slowly tense, then relax, muscles in different parts of your body.

Find healthy ways to manage anger.

- Make a list of things that trigger your anger. For example, these could include feeling ignored, being criticized or being in traffic jams.
- Recognize when you are getting angry. Your muscles may get tense and your jaw may clench. You may start breathing faster, or raise your voice.
- If you feel yourself getting angry, stop what you are doing.
- Count slowly to 10 to try to calm down.
- Walk away from the person or situation that is making you angry, if you can.
- If possible, go for a walk and don't come back until you have calmed down. (Don't leave your child unsupervised).
- Call someone in your support network to talk it out. See page 29.

Get enough physical activity.

- Get at least 150 minutes of moderate—or 75 minutes of vigorous—physical activity each week.
- For greater health benefits, get at least 300 minutes of moderate—or 150 minutes of vigorous—physical activity each week.
- Try to spread your activity throughout the week, getting at least 10 minutes at a time.
- In addition, do muscle strengthening exercises at least 2 days each week.

Consult your health-care provider before starting an exercise program.

Create a healthy eating pattern.

- Know how many daily calories are right for your gender, age and activity level. Having more calories will lead to weight gain.
- Find out what's in your food and drinks—check Nutrition Facts labels and ingredients. Limit items high in calories, saturated or trans fats, sodium, cholesterol and added sugars. Choose more whole grains.
- Build a healthy plate—fill half with fruits and vegetables.
- Drink more low-fat or fat-free milk.
- Choose lean cuts of meat. Eat seafood at least twice a week.
- Limit sweetened drinks to help cut calories.
- Cook more at home so you are in charge of what's in your food. Use small amounts of vegetable oils, when needed, in place of butter or other solid fats. And add little salt or sugar.
- Avoid oversized portions, and don't eat in front of the TV you'll eat more.

Avoid alcohol and other drugs.

They don't help you cope with problems and only make things worse. In addition, they could land you back in prison. You could also be putting the time you spend with your child at risk.

- Follow any guidelines in your pre-release plan about getting treatment or support for substance abuse.
- If you think you might have a problem with alcohol or other drugs and would like to get help, contact the Center for Substance Abuse Treatment's Referral Service at
  1-800-662-HELP
  (1-800-662-4357) or visit
  www.findtreatment.samhsa.gov.

YOU ARE NOT ALONE.

Support and advice are available to help you be the best parent you can be while you're in prison and after you get out. Sources include:

Your support network

These are people who are trustworthy and dependable people whose judgment you trust. They are people you can turn to when you need help or advice. Members of your support network could include:

- friends
- family members
- community groups
- spiritual leaders

State and local services

These could include:

- health clinics or healthcare providers
- social and family services
- hotlines
- the extension service in your state

Check the community service number in the front section of your phone book.

Your probation or parole officer

He or she may be able to connect you to sources of help.

National organizations

- Administration for Children and Families U.S. Department of Health and Human Services www.acf.hhs.gov

- American Academy of Pediatrics www.healthychildren.org

- Childhelp® National Child Abuse Hotline
  1-800-4-A-CHILD
  (1-800-422-4453)

- Prevent Child Abuse America]
  1-800-CHILDREN
  (1-800-244-5373)
  www.preventchildabuse.org

- National Domestic Violence Hotline 1-800-799-SAFE
  (1-800-799-7233)
  (English and Spanish)
  1-800-787-3224 (TTY)

Who is in your support network?

List their names and phone numbers below

_____

_____

_____

_____

_____

_____

_____

_____

_____

_____

_____

_____

_____

_____

_____

_____

_____

_____

_____

_____

_____

_____

_____

_____

_____

STAY INVOLVED ON YOUR CHILD'S LIFE.
Remember, a prison sentence doesn't stop you from being a parent.

Do what you can while in prison.

- Stay in regular contact with your child through letters and phone calls.
- Work on keeping a good relationship with your child's caregiver.
- If possible, ask the caregiver to bring your child for visits.
- Take advantage of any programs at your facility that let you record audio and video messages for your child.

Focus on being a better parent when you're released.

- Set goals for yourself, and make a plan to reach them.
- Spend as much time as you can with your child.
- Avoid old habits, friends and situations that could get you in trouble again.
- Build a support network and reach out for help when you need it.

It's never too late to make positive changes in your life!

Made in the USA
Middletown, DE
19 February 2022

61524321R00020